"I Do"s (and Don'ts)

"I Do"s (and Don'ts)

Advice, and Poetry, for the Newly
Engaged, and for those Contemplating,
and Practicing, the Married Life

Joseph Byrd

iUniverse, Inc.
New York Lincoln Shanghai

"I Do"s (and Don'ts)

Advice, and Poetry, for the Newly Engaged, and for those Contemplating, and Practicing, the Married Life

iUniverse books may be ordered through booksellers or by contacting:

iUniverse
2021 Pine Lake Road, Suite 100
Lincoln, NE 68512
www.iuniverse.com
1-800-Authors (1-800-288-4677)

ISBN-13: 978-0-595-39575-0 (pbk)
ISBN-13: 978-0-595-83977-3 (ebk)
ISBN-10: 0-595-39575-9 (pbk)
ISBN-10: 0-595-83977-0 (ebk)

Printed in the United States of America

For
Ryan Winningham and Amie Senyk

and for
Jennica Skoug

"The essential conditions of everything you do must be choice, love, and passion…."

Nadia Boulanger

"The tragedy of life is what dies in a person while he or she lives."

Albert Schweitzer

Foreword

My wife and I received the following marriage counseling, from a Catholic priest and an Eritrean Lutheran pastor, respectively:

1) Drink a glass of wine each month on the day of your anniversary, and

2) Remember: children can come at any time.

Mind you, we sought no more than this terse, though effective, advice. Be it arrogant or not, we felt strongly about one thing at the beginning of our relationship: the strength of our married life was our own. No one person, and certainly no one institution, could impart the kind of detailed instruction that would make or break the covenant we were about to enter. Marriage counseling cannot be tallied or condensed to something more or less effective, and, as every couple is certainly and most blessedly unique, neither should it.

Nonetheless, many newlyweds (indeed, many long-married couples as well), want answers. In a day when marriage vows are regarded as less than truly solemn promises, couples embarking through the desert of engagement (after reveling in the verdant valleys of courtship) seek answers; advice to guide them, certainly through the time prior to the ceremony itself, and, hopefully, thereafter. There are answers to be had, in a sense, as long as these answers are allowed to daily check themselves against their own self-created consistencies. And, as marriage is an end-lessly changing, eternally permanent reality (and as a foolish consistency is the hobgoblin of little minds), answers have their place within this scheme.

What follows is what has worked for us. And what, I imagine, will continue to work, for as the saying goes, so far, so good. It has been so good for us. May this book help it to be better for you, too.

—JB

PS—I've interspersed poetry between each section as both speed bump and intermission. The poems, hopefully, will invite you to take a break from the sometimes mind-numbing continuum of advice *ad nauseam*. In other words, don't read too much of this book in one sitting. Take your time, and let it soak in. And let the poetry speak to the many facets of marriage: serious, goofy, earthy, sublime; deep, and not-so-deep. If some of these poems don't make you laugh, or cry, or at least take pause, then I haven't done my job. Good marriage is about being alive, and if the advice doesn't help you feel that way, hopefully the poetry will.

Warning

Advice only works when it works, and ideals are important points of discussion, not sociological yardsticks against which to measure yourselves. This book is full of both, and if your relationship is able to match its impossibly high standards, then you're either in such deep denial that counseling is immediately recommended, or you're not of this earth. We're all working toward better marriages, and this book invites you to join in the fun, and do the same.

~Your wedding is not your own. It is a community event and a family rite, and it can be a test of your compatibility. If you don't desire these things, elope.

Parents have this odd, historical habit of involving themselves in the weddings of their children. And children seem strangely surprised when these parental ideas and desires conflict with their image of what will or will not happen before and after the altar.

Whose wedding is it anyway?

In fact, your wedding belongs to everyone. Scaling the marriage mountain is a team effort, and rightly so. It is a rite of passage (one of the few that remain in our fast-food world), and it can be a meaningful exit from the life that formed you.

You may, of course, choose to fight this sometimes volcanic force, attempting to impede the magma of familial marriage opinion and involvement. The mountain, however, will most likely have its way. It's best to go along with the flow, whenever possible. Decide what is important to you, and what is not. If you care about the color and type of flower used, but not at all about the brand of butter mints, make this known to the mountain, and move on. If the styling of the wedding program is your *raison d'être*, but you couldn't be bothered with details of photographic memorabilia, then let it be so. You will win, and learn, from this give and take, for such is the practice of good marriage.

Parents mean well, usually. And even if they don't, consider your geological scars a Marriage Aptitude Test of the first order, your score simply being pass, or fail.

If you opt to skip this test, and elope, you can be certain that various MAT's will surface sooner rather than later. Married life is filled with mountains and valleys that will outscale the seeming massif of the wedding ceremony, and it's never too soon to prepare for future tests.

Besides, nothing is more rewarding than having a buddy with whom to study.

"I am my beloved's, and my beloved is mine."

The Song of Songs

Music students get married

We ate waffles the night that we met; sweet,
grainy things. They told what would come: a life
that's moved from state to state, that's held no treat
but each other's company, often rife
with practice-rooms and metronomes, with queens
of mind games and of teaching—women full
in their need to control (but how our spleens
tickled at the learning, the music's pull).
And though we've steamed ourselves a bit, and pressed
what once was fluid into squares, left stuck
some skin on these hot snags, who could have guessed
the sweetness of these injuries, the luck
of this, our meal: the syrup's ours to pour.
The decadence of our love flows, grows more.

~Marriage is part of the order of creation. Your wedding service isn't.

The music you do, or do not, select for your wedding ceremony; the license you will sign; the gowns, the groomsmen, the seating of parents and grandparents: all these have little to do with the truth of that moment when you seal yourselves to each other for all time. The wedding service is about redemption, fidelity, and epic journey. Your marriage permanently inscribes these ideals on your hearts, and nothing you do or say can add or detract from them.

At the same time, don't take the service too seriously. It's just a snapshot in the photo album of your life. As nice as it would be to think that the trappings of your wedding are fresh and original, they aren't. But you are, and that's all that matters.

Be aware, however, of becoming your own Marriage Vortex. Are you shocked when the soloist isn't interested in arranging a meeting so that you might hear how she sounds? Do your groomsman visibly squirm when asked to get that fitting at the tux shop, a year before the wedding? Is the organist not returning your phone calls? Could it be that this is the 794th wedding that he has accompanied in his life (many of which he has been poorly compensated for, if at all), and one more nuptial ceremony under his belt means very little to him, relatively speaking? Is the photographer charging an arm and a leg? Is it possible that her fees include the necessary professionalism required to maneuver a sea of pushy mothers-in-law who command what will and will not be photographed? Will the pastor not allow rice or birdseed to be thrown as you enter your carriage or limousine, perhaps because he is the one who will be left there sweeping it up before the arrival of fussy church ladies the following morning, who will be more than happy to give him a piece of their cranky minds?

The Justice of the Peace is always an option. Or, just get married, and let the wild kaleidoscope of events and details swirl around you in titular array, deliciously out of focus next to the sharply defined beauty of the vows you make on that day.

"If a man has recently married, he must not be sent to war or have any other duty laid on him. For one year he is to be free to stay at home and bring happiness to the wife he has married."

Deuteronomy 24:5

Dearly beloved

There are XL pews here and
eyes larger than that, bulging in and out of their
light bulb sockets, sizing up the sizable rears that
scoot across in politeness, warmly and coldly shifting down the row,
slightly moist in good, sweaty, Christian posture.
Pachelbel shoots off his canon and the race begins,
female-like bridal accessory maids precipitating from dark corners in
billowing gray gowns like spring rain clouds gathering for a storm.
The weather breaks, the trumpet hits a fat note, and the
bride rolls in like a white Southern California Cadillac on
adjustable hydraulic struts, pews shaking slightly as she thunders
toward her black-breasted groom, who stares up at the ceiling fan
above, whirring like a three-spoked Trinitarian iris, watching over this
love feast.
Daddy gives his daughterly Divinity away with a voice not unlike the
Good Humor man,
wheeling his white sweet cart into hitching position, lovers extending
moist hand to moist hand like a human double-stuffed Oreo, the join-
ing of which no one dares speak against.
It's scripture time and the bride's shimmering, well-busted mother
hoists herself into the pulpit, speaking in large, round vowels of love,
and gongs.
Pronouncing them one flesh,
one hotdog in one bun,
one onion in one beer-battered ring,
one roast,
The Rev. prays: *bring them to the table, Lord,*
where your saints feast forever
in their eternal home.
The crowd murmurs in pleasure,
and the life-long reception begins.

~Have no expectations of each other.

You are a child waiting for a party. You've been promised cake, balloons, games, and sweets. The backyard will be filled with friends, and the party starts at 3 PM. With six torturous hours to wait, you sit in the kitchen, moon-eyed, drumming your fingers on the tabletop.

At 3 PM, as the clock strikes (in fact, just as the clock begins to strike), you jump from your seat and race to the back door, flinging it wide, only to find a single, sagging balloon, and a slice of half-eaten cake. A trail of ants winds toward the melting strawberry ice cream which has begun to soak through the paper plate. Your mouth opens and your stomach drops. Your expectations have been shattered, and your heart is broken. This is the same way many marriages begin.

False ideas and impossible scenarios of what our marriages should be like can infect us through the well-intentioned talk of friends and family, through our own unfulfilled inadequacies, through images from the media. We learn to expect things to be the way we've seen them, the way we've been told they should be. With this self-draughted poison we sicken our spousal relationships, desiring to get what we've been told we'll get. This house of cards always falls, and we always end up with deflated, dripping, ant-filled marriages when expectations rule our relationships.

But when we invite our spouses to be themselves, letting them feel how they feel (not telling them, or expecting them, to have certain emotions about certain things), we open the door to a different kind of party, one that grows richer each day. Expectations of any kind, no matter how well-founded they may seem, are relational jail cells. Most marital unhappiness stems from their unnecessary existence.

Clear away, daily, through conversation, and through meditation, all the images you've accumulated of how husbands and wives *should* behave. There are no 'shoulds' in marriage. Anyone can come along and say how things should be, but it takes love and patience to see how things *are*, to work with them, and through them. That's marriage. Waiting for things to be different, or better, because they should be, is not marriage. It is hell.

Expectations, however, are not the same as requirements, and every relationship has its necessary set of the same.

"A good relationship has a pattern like a dance and is built on some of the same rules. The partners do not need to hold on tightly because they move frequently in the same pattern, intricate but gay, and swift and free.... The joy of such a pattern is not only the joy of creation but the joy of participation. It is also the joy of living in the moment. Lightness of touch and living in the moment are intertwined."

Anne Morrow Lindbergh

What you've been asking for/writing in the airport lounge

Our love is written
in your red and white checkered 1st grade dress,
its smell,
and how your young name pokes
from the photograph's back.
G on your cheek,
R, your top button.

Our love stands as a
Ferris wheel, revolving.
A tall one.
It is written there on
each spoke,
some in lights,
some in canceled postage stamps, the words they carried.
Each passing basket whispers,
embraces:
There is no line here.
There is no gate to it.
No need.

Our love tastes like a
Rueben sandwich.
Tuneful, glorious, decadent and tangy.
Rich.
Our love stands as a grill.
Solid,
heavy, and
one piece.
A sizzling, greased bed.

Ours is me at my
self-made airport suitcase poetry table,
or my mother's laugh when you asked
writin' me a long love poem? and I said
no, but I'll start right away.

Ours is this,
your first.
Mine, too.
The bottle has opened.

~Expectations are not the same as requirements, and every relationship has its necessary set of the same.

A documentary on public television showed a pair of baby monkeys in separate cages. One, allowed two hours a day of contact with its mother, thrived. The other, denied any motherly contact, though food and water were in plenty, died. Humans are no different. Our relationships die when they lose their nurturing, sustaining qualities, which include:

- Touch that is loving, generous and consistent; consistent inasmuch as the 'touch' of your words is in harmony with that of your hands. Tough talk during the day makes tenderness unlikely at night.

- Freedom. Let there be both emotional and physical space between you daily in small amounts, and let your longer occasional spaces be points of discussion and discovery. Plenty of couples deem their antipathy toward separateness as relational gold, when it is anything but. You go together where you go alone, but you mold together when there is no coming or going.

- Encouragement. Encourage each other in all ways and at all times. Be daring and ridiculous in how supportive you are of one another. Free yourselves, as well, from being critical. There is never a need, except vengeance, to tear one another down.

Touch, freedom and encouragement are elemental to relational well-being. Like earth, sun, and water, they work together, creating both balance and growth.

> "But let there be spaces in your togetherness, and let the winds of the heavens dance between you."
>
> Kahlil Gibran

At your concert, writing in the balcony

I'm perched up here, a gargoyle without sight,
a stone-tongued gutter-spout who'd rather see
than gurgle words and rhymes that never right
themselves into a page of poetry,
my granite spirit stuck within this pen.
I hear you playing on the stage, and think
how many times I've heard, and will again,
your notes ascending up, while my words sink.
Yet in these thoughts myself almost despising
I hear the children of our musics meet:
mine, liquid words; yours, songs from earth arising,
an intercourse of sounds that helps defeat
this demon with its claws around my heart.
And once again you've saved me by your art.

~Don't let your career interfere with your marriage

Who do you love? Your spouse, or your career?

Yes, the choice is that severe, for a few reasons:

- Be clear about your career dreams. If they don't involve your marriage in a healthy way, don't get married. Or, choose a new career about which to dream, and be creative. Often, the most satisfying careers are those which allow your marriage to thrive.

- Careers can be used as weapons, sadly. What was once a viable means of maintaining financial (and emotional) stability can quickly become an emotional bludgeoning stick, the 'bread winner' acting as if he, or she, is more important than the other. This drama is more common than not, and it is a sham. Marriages are equal partnerships, not business mergers.

- Often, as marriages cool, careers heat up. With promotions or increased responsibilities come feelings of prestige or worth. Don't substitute these temporal moments of self-esteem for the ongoing goodness and real emotional value of a healthy marriage. Your career will pass away. Your marriage never will.

- When money becomes more important than your relationship, things go awry. Don't let this happen. Remember the simplicity of your first days together when, hopefully, the only important thing was just that: you were together.

- The amount of time you spend at work can easily supersede the amount spent with your spouse. To use a tired, but true, phrase, make your at-home time 'quality time,' and let your work time be the vehicle for this quality.

- The ins and outs of careers can be stressful. If possible, set a time-limit for discussing the day's muck. 20 minutes is good, 10 minutes even better. More than that sets up your daily goings on as an altar of negativity toward which you are increasingly drawn, lessening your positive time with each other.

Remember: there are sacrifices to be made in marriage. Careers and their related necessities can be one of them. Your relationship, however, should not suffer, nor be sacrificed, for your career.

"It is quite impossible to be happily married to another if one does not first get a divorce from oneself."

Anthony De Mello

~~~

A cup of water
brought in the night with love can
be a joy to both

(read Sheldon Van Auken's *A Severe Mercy*)

~Allow your sexual relationship to be simple and sincere, and let it grow with you. Let no image from the media define your sexuality as a couple.

Sex is powerful. It makes babies. It feels good, and it's supposed to. It's also one of the 'big three' problem areas in marriages, (the other two being money, and career).

The often touted idea of 'sexual compatibility' is a farce. Don't believe it. You have no need to take a 'test drive' before marriage, to see if it 'works' between you. Of course it will. That doesn't mean, however, that everything will be perfect. Sex is messy, actually. It strikes deeply at those parts of yourself that are the most vulnerable and the most intense. And it keeps us human, thank goodness.

If, after you're married, all goes well—congratulations! Enjoy yourselves, and grow together. If it doesn't, for whatever reason, talk to someone you trust. In any case, remember:

- Allow yourselves the privilege of being initiates. Treat each other as newly discovered works of living art. Ponder each other. Let each time be special.

- Don't listen to braggarts or sexual story-tellers. There are lots of them out there, especially on television and in the movies. It's all fantasy, and you have something much better: a living, breathing spouse to love and cherish. Don't compare yourselves to anyone else. It only causes problems.

- Contraception is great, except that it contradicts what sex is all about. With so many couples experiencing infertility issues, don't take for granted the power of conceiving a family. Don't let anyone else tell you what you should do about it either.

- Beware of this idea of 'sensational sex' which lots of self-help books claim it is possible to have. Yes; knowledge is power, and can help very much when it comes to intimacy, but a little bit goes a long way. Gentleness and sensitivity, for which there is no substitute, are what will make your sex life truly sensational.

- Keep your words kind and your practice patient, at all times and in all settings, and you will save yourselves from unnecessary heartache. It's easy to say or do something hurtful in the intensity of the moment.

- Give yourselves time. It can take years to understand each other's bodies. Do not allow the whimsies of schedule to dictate the means or the methods of your love making.

- Sense the moment, and respond in kind. Anything more than this is not love. Anything less than this is not human.

"Die, where thou hast lived; Quicken with kissing; had my lips that power, Thus would I wear them out."

Shakespeare (Cleopatra, to the dying Antony)

July 4th 1995

We picked blueberries for money
15¢ per pound
bonus for late-stayers: 5¢

We wore cheap straw hats
We tied white buckets to our waists

We separated each bush
lifting the leg of a low branch
gently
its length
        smooth
arched
      until the
blue cluster
hung there
           swaying

We picked with
slow
cupped hands
        rolled each berry to
drop
in
the buckets
      between our legs

We offered the biggest berries
to each other
made delicious sounds
like a flock of
feasting birds

They
fired
the starling canon
startling the little birds
and us
        shocked by the
freedom
of our love

~Let no resentment come between you. When it does, talk about it. If you can't talk about it, learn to do so. If you can't learn to do so, don't get married.

Bitterness and resentment of any kind spell trouble for all relationships, young and old. And as it takes maturity, and some learning, to employ the skills of healthy, ongoing communication, the small but insidious seeds of anger are easily scattered onto the soil of even the most well-tended marriages.

This little book is not the place to discuss the skills of healthy communication, but know this: if you let the sun set on your anger a few times, and multiply these evenings of ire by five or ten years, you will awaken one morning married to your own misery. The more your resentment builds, the less you are aware that the misery you're experiencing is your own fault, not your spouse's. It may feel right, even good, to blame him or her for what has become of your marriage, but your resentment is never your spouse's fault, and as blaming never solved a thing, you are the one in the wrong.

It is the ones we love most and are the closest to that we first begin to kill, the strongest poison flowing from the least of our sideways looks, our off-putting gestures, and our small, critical innuendoes.

Hiding your resentment is a kind of adultery: in love with your own anger, you treasure and nurse its secret, pulsing space more than you treasure your spouse. Talk, talk, talk, until death parts you, and let every word be the truth, and spoken in love.

Let it out, or let it go. If you can't do either, don't get married.

A POISON TREE

I was angry with my friend:
I told my wrath, my wrath did end.
I was angry with my foe:
I told it not, my wrath did grow.

And I watered it in fears
Night and morning with my tears,
And I sunned it with smiles
And with soft deceitful wiles.

And it grew both day and night,
Till it bore an apple bright,
And my foe beheld it shine,
And he knew that it was mine,

And into my garden stole
When the night had veiled the pole;
In the morning, glad, I see
My foe outstretched beneath the tree.

(*Songs of Experience*, William Blake)

Love at first sound

I sat in a balcony while you warmed
up to play for mass, thinking "Let's see how
she handles this old organist" (who'd stormed
upstairs like some sacred Catholic cow).
It was pure falconry: the way his hawk-
like humor and his biting, snide remarks
lit on your kind hands. He couldn't out-talk
you, so he tried outplaying you. The sparks
flew from his pipes, your fingers touched your strings.
I still remember how it felt to hear
your viola that first, sweet time, how round
and full; how you endowed his noise with wings.
I knew I'd have to fly to you, too, dear.
That's why I believe in love at first sound.

~Schedule monthly 'State of the Relationship' meetings.

Regularly discuss these questions with each other:

- What is the one thing I like best about myself?

- What is the one thing I like least about myself?

- What is the one thing you like most about me?

- What is the one thing you like least about me?

- How do our families affect our relationship for the good? For the bad?

- What are my expectations about sex?

- What are your expectations about household duties?

- How does money affect our relationship? How does it affect the balance of power in our relationship?

- How do you see children affecting our relationship? What will your role be in taking care of them?

- Where do you see yourself in 10 years? In 20?

- Where do you see us in 10 years? In 20?

- If you could change one thing about yourself, what would it be?

- If you could change one thing about me, what would it be?

- On a scale of one to ten, one being the least and ten the most, how enjoyable is our relationship, and why?

- What couples in our life can we learn from by their positive/negative example?

- How do you see geography affecting our relationship? i.e. where would you like to live; how close to family would you like to be; what places appeal, disappeal to you?

"'Woman,' Eve said. 'I am woman and you are man.' 'She speaks just like I do,' Adam thought.'

—Traditional Jewish

Eve

That singing snake crowded all her knowing
green and glistening in his flowing, sequined smoking jacket, crooning
lithely
s'wonderful
      s'marvelous
until she cared
           for him
until that moist mouth of ages proffered its
divinely designed velvet e-z chair
      as humid home to His homemade apple crisp,
and she won:
              first loser of a miss universe pageant
              first deliberate vegetarian
              first shy nudist of the colony
              first underwear seamstress
              first scapegoat, first buck-passer
              first mother of a rotten child
              first mourner of a premature funeral
              first farmer's wife of this garden grown wild

~Children are a gift, not a right.

Children can come at any time.

Children do not come at all, sometimes.

Children do not require garbage disposals, three-car garages, separate rooms, or mini-vans.

Children do require touch, freedom, and encouragement. Diapers help, too.

Children cry.

Children take time.

Children are not as expensive as the world would have you think.

Children practice mercy and forgiveness daily and without guile. Learn from their example.

Children are born loving to sing and dance. Fill your time together with the same: your toil will seem trivial, and your playtime will have a positive power that lasts through your years together.

Children will change your life forever, whether you like it or not.

Children grow up quickly. Read books, take walks, play together, and hold each other as often as you possibly can.

Children are not weekend playthings. Placing them in day-care during the week, so that you can afford your life by working full-time, is nonsense. Choose children or choose full-time work. Choosing both is simply selfishness.

Children are an unflinching portrait of the summation of your behavior. If you don't like your children, blame yourself, not them.

Children, however, are not a report card of your parenting skills. They are their own people, often at an earlier age than we suspect.

Children will not always do what you want.

Children, however, need to know what you expect from them. Your consistency in communicating this means everything.

Children need guidance, not control. Guided children come to you first when seeking help and advice. Controlled children look elsewhere, hiding their concerns altogether, sometimes to the point of duplicity.

Children are not created in your image. They may look like you, but they are not you. Do not expect them to become anything other than the delightfully unique individuals they are. If you have controlled them, their uniqueness will irk you. If you have guided them, you will revel in it.

Children will expose, and quickly, the weaknesses in your marriage. Do not blame them for this. Learn from it.

Children are not prescriptions for failing marriages.

Children instantly sense favoritism.

Children should be children as long as possible. The world will curtail their childhood soon enough.

Children have a right to make their own choices when raising their own children. Interfering in this process, without their consent, is bad form on your part.

Children will choose spouses with personalities similar to your own. Support their choices, or risk alienating them.

Children are not implicitly required to take care of you in your old age.

Children will be better spouses when reasonably allowed to witness the process of your conflicts and your resolutions with each other.

Children are more sensitive to the emotional goings on of your marriage than you might suspect.

Children need as much freedom as you can give them. Their need for this occurs incrementally, and your awareness of it is vital to both their sense of confidence and their emotional health.

Children will make you hear and see the learned legacy of your own parents. For the most part, you will treat your children the same way your parents treated you. It takes thorough self-examination and considerable will power to change this, if you so desire. Counseling and/or therapy can help, too.

~~~

"Why can't they be like we were, perfect in every way? What's the matter with kids today?"

from *Bye Bye Birdie*

A musician father advises

There's a head shaking in the front room.
It's Beatrice, and it's Bartók playing.
I want to warn her 7½ month brain as she
crouches, laughing, lunging just to fall:
Beware.
Love music as you would a
trashcan of cabbage left in the summer sun.
It nourishes. It's rich. And it permeates, but it can
cut you in half, and
crucify you in the daily practice room.
You will set up banquets in your mind,
halls of feasting, song, revelry, and delight.
But when you open the door to the great room
you had supposed in your baby Bartók brain
and it's 8 by 8 with a beaten, scarred piano in the corner and a
gray folding chair for a bench, a gaping vent above it
reeking softly with the sweet smell of aged trash,
you, too, will shake your head
not in rhythm
but in the wonder of dismay:
this is my life
this room and the sounds I make, are
my feast of delight
my meal of bread, vinegar, and bones, in
this the great hall of my necessary undoing.
I will halve my ears and cut them in pieces
and nail the pieces to these dirty brown walls
and
listen to what sounds I'm hearing as I
play for myself,
myself, myself.

And someday, you might hear what I've heard, too,
and it just might be
in a great room, followed, perhaps, by a
delight-filled feast of bread and old, red wine, on bone china.
But only perhaps, and absolutely only after
hours of days and weeks full of years in the room with the ears on the
dirty brown walls.
So be it, if the music calls.
But be sure it's the music.
Be sure it is the music that
calls you there to the room with the sweet, rotting air.

~A divorce isn't an event, it's a process.

Divorce doesn't just fall from the sky. It is the result of relational delinquency; the gradual mortification of a marriage, with all its accompanying signs: lack of physical and emotional intimacy, loss of tenderness, poor communication, hostility. Do not brush any of these off as phases or flukes. Fight them at their first sign, and do it with love and compassion.

Divorce is an illusion. You can not be separated, except by death, from someone to whom you have vowed eternal love and faithfulness. You can live separately, marry others, maintain distance of all kinds, but there is no divorcing what has been made whole forever. The wounds of divorce can heal, but the scars will always remain tender.

Sadly, most severed marriages were long in the throes of this progressive demise before the idea of divorce became a reality.

Unless you are undergoing abuse, adultery, or other atrocities of neglect, there is no reason for divorce, and anything else is an excuse to abandon the truth: that you, too, took part in allowing this relationship to die.

"Stop blaming other people, and you will feel what an alcoholic feels when he stops drinking, or what a smoker feels when he stops smoking. You will feel that you have brought relief to your soul."

Leo Tolstoy

After a phone call/this is me

When I talk to you
cougars lick my kneecaps
growling:
          this
is you
this is you
this
is you
Do not tell your teeth lies
Do not taste your lying teeth
Do not betray your first mouth
It knows better

~Do not allow your marriage to grow stale

Read a book together.

Keep a diary of all the funny things that you notice in each other. Read it occasionally.

Serve ice cream for lunch.

Take a drive in the middle of a rainstorm.

Sleep together in a different room.

Go to the stationers and choose cards you would give each other. Don't buy them.

Get rid of the TV.

Walk in the woods and hold hands the entire time.

Go on a picnic.

Buy automatic cars so you can hold hands while driving.

Live in a foreign country together.

Fold each other's laundry.

Keep a calendar of special moments you've had together.

Help someone in need anonymously.

Choose married friends who exhibit positive, loving relationships.

Sit around a fire together.

Sing together.

Feed each other dinner.

Exercise together.

Open the curtains, turn off the lights, and watch a thunderstorm.

Go to a baseball game and, if possible, sit in the grass.

Order for each other at a restaurant.

Choose a double bed so that nighttime cuddling is a given.

Take the train whenever possible.

Find a star chart and learn constellations together.

Sleep naked as often as possible.

Go camping.

Rent a tandem bicycle.

Write letters to one another to be opened upon your next anniversary.

Cook together.

Choose a weekly 'date night.'

Drink a glass of wine on the day of your anniversary each month.

Bathe together.

Take a vacation during the winter.

Go dog sledding.

Take a class together.

Make each other breakfast in bed.

Take your picture together in front of the capitol buildings of all 50 states.

Open a road atlas, choose a place you've never been to, and go there.

Plant a garden together.

Have children.

~~~

When you bite jicama with a fake chomp
as if it were an apple; when you rip
the soles off your tennis shoes and then stomp
through the house, squealing "slippers!"; when you tip
the waitress far more than she's worth; when you
turn down the sound of my Handel CD
and then blast the windows out with your new
ABBA album: these are the things that free
me—mute prisoner of my homemade rules,
a self-caged bird, clipped and songless, gasping
for tunes that used to mean something, for schools
books, teachers—something besides this rasping,
this sound of nothing. But when I watch you,
a hope fills my throat, my wings spread anew.

~Shared theology does not necessarily assure a successful marriage.

Many couples of Muslim, Hindu, Buddhist, Jewish, Christian, and other faiths are successfully married.

Many of the same are divorced.

Though it can certainly be both a starting point and a strengthener of relationships, compatible theology is no guarantee of compatible marriage.

Many are the conversations my wife has overheard in coffee houses where a woman shares far too many details of how hard she has worked to bring her husband back to God. As if one can leave God in the first place.

Many are the husbands I have seen putting on a 'tough-guy' act, attempting thereby to separate themselves from the innate spirituality of their marriages. Too late. 'So long as you both shall live' is about as serious an invitation to the Divine as there ever was. You can't uninvite God, though you may try.

Many are the couples who force themselves through daily devotions, straining to find a common theology, fretting over the details of religiosity. God can't be gotten, or boxed up. Neither can your relationship.

There is more mystery in the daily working out of your married life than in any systematized religious necessity which you have either been trained in or forced to believe. But make no mistake: shared theology can be the strongest of footholds as you climb the mountain together. Just don't let your feet get stuck. Keep climbing, and keep growing. And believe that God can, and will, do far greater things in your lives than you could ever imagine. That is, if you let him, and if you trust in the simplicity of what you said to each other on that day you committed to this journey of compassion.

Don't let religion interfere with the spirituality of your marriage.

"Here lyes a shee Sunne, and a hee Moone here,
She gives the best light to his Spheare,
Or each is both, and all, and so,
They unto one another nothing owe..."

John Donne

In church/thinking of dogs

I love dogs and I speak their language;
their kindergarten cackle at one, free-tongued lick-me session,
their howlelujah when communing at the chow dish,
their pink-gummed delight, holy water slobbering over
someone new,
their lovely, lanky, witness wiggle: I ruff rou

This is the way we might better be,
with chewed up hymnals, paper flecks stuck in our mouth folds,
a corner for doo doo, and it stays there only
(not smeared on others, not hidden behind nicely talked sentence
sweets, stinking,
not shovel flung over back fence meetings),
deeply dug holy holes for biblical bones,
(words are meaningless to an empty stomach)
and a panting, rough-breathed, leash-breaking need to
sniff everyone and everything.
Everywhere.

~Marriage is not a 50-50 situation.

"Marriage is not a 50-50 situation. Each person must feel they are giving 90 percent."

(John A., married 35 years)

"You've just gotta give up for each other, and you gotta know when the other person needs more givin'. It always works out, but you just gotta keep givin' up for each other."

(Vivian H., married 65 years)

"Don't put up barriers. Keep listening."

(Sheila D., married 12 years)

"If you don't have a sense of humor with and for each other, you may as well forget about it."

(Brenda O., married 20 years)

"It's sex. If it weren't for the fact that Brenda's a woman, I could just as well be married to my best friend Paul."

(John O., married 20 years)

"You know what the secret is? Forgiveness. I'm convinced of it."

(Mary O., married 50 years)

Molly: "We solve all our problems together."
Mary: "Oh brother. That would be hard."
Molly: "It is hard, but it works. It brings you closer together."

(Molly Z., married 17 years)

"I don't know. The Lord. Is that a good answer? [*laughs*] Lots of prayer [*laughs more*]. He goes to work, I stay home."

(Shelley P., married 20 years)

"Be able to start over when necessary."

(Tim G., married 12 years)

"Pick the right person."

(Andrew J., married 12 years)

I've known redemption

By the Siegesäule
one Chinese man
asked for one picture
asked in English
and if you haven't known it
English speaks sweetest in Berlin

I declined
spoke auf Deutsch
said
too hurried, spät and
his face burned my mind's hand
as a precious medallion
retrieved from a bed of coals

Now
it's Holland's Schiphol airport
one other Chinese man asks
picture please
in front of that fantastically gorgeous
ordinary flower bed
and I dropped this pen in my
hurriedness for him

click
thanks and my retrieved pen
scuffs at my paper like a
tap dancer with a loose screw

I write this cheap poem
the pen works again
the sun even busts in beams through the clouds
first time today

this
is a true poem

coda: the bike rider behind me
        stopped for Chinese man #1
        her name: Grace
        how do I know: my wife

~You may lead by example, living by the book, doing and saying all the correct, loving things, but your spouse may not respond in kind.

There is no shortage of literature and information on the nature of marriage; the fixing of ailing marriages; the differences between men and women in marriage; the disheartening statistics of failed marriages. It overwhelms and it confuses, and, as love is a many splendored thing, no one book has all the answers.

What publishing firms, talk-show hosts, and self-help mavens want to keep mum is that books will not necessarily clear the fog that can sometimes settle on the structures of your wedded life. What will lift the haze is the ongoing practice of mercy and love, applied in ways that speak to your spouse, though they may not be how you would choose to be loved. Only you can do this, and only you know how. Each marriage is unique, and no book can prescribe the necessary Rx for your love life, if you have, in fact, lost that loving feeling.

The truths in your relationship, those elements that form the back-bone of how well you do and don't work together, will wither if taken too seriously, if held relentlessly under the microscope of the latest pop psychology. Relaxing into the mercy and joy that first brought you together is a profounder exercise than running the gauntlet of marriage-saving techniques found in every bookstore on the planet. In other words, all you need is love.

Books can help clarify situations and ideas for the reader, though the reader is usually not the one who needs help. And nothing is more potentially dangerous to a relationship than when one person, armed with a battery of how-to books, decides to fix what is wrong with the marriage. The other feels that he or she is in a menagerie, or under construction, or under attack.

Make love, not war.

"Let me not to the marriage of true minds
Admit impediments. Love is not love
Which alters when it alteration finds,
Or bends with the remover to remove:
O no! It is an ever fixed mark."

Shakespeare

Waiting for the rehearsal to be over

It's been highways and it's been circles these five years with her:
tarred parking lot cracks;
black-scuffed bathroom doors;
expensive lamps on crappy green tables with sign-in sheets;
these three returning, continually, in Rochester, Berlin, Kalamazoo,
at auditions, in *hochschules*, at rehearsals, going, waiting, writing.
But for one dollar and some corny cents today
one book from the cheap store helps me see it all clear:
I am
asleep
in a dying mall's car lot, and I can smell the
tar—it's hot in my life here—and I had to
go in a bad bathroom between dead stores down a
dirty hallway with kicked doors, only to
listen to Strauss bellowers upon returning to the hopeful radio
in my close car next to
Plymouth's dotted with children in polka clothes
rental trucks with sweaty sandwiches bulging
and sides of gravel-flavored cole slaw

are there sacrifices in marriage
are there sacrifices in marriage

are there sacrifices in marriage

cracks are the growth
doors are of hope
tables are for the future
but these words came from my eyes
and one day
I
will
open them

~It's not who you can live with, it's who you can't live without

If you can imagine yourself not marrying your fiancée, don't get married.

If your heart doesn't jump every time he walks through the door, don't get married.

If you find yourself attracted to anyone else during your courtship and engagement, and/or if you notice the same in your fiancée, don't get married.

If you don't want to spend the rest of your life learning, don't get married.

If little things, like toilet seats and tooth paste caps, bug you, don't get married.

If you think your fiancé will change once you are married, don't get married.

If you want to change your fiancée in any way, don't get married.

If something bugs you about your fiancé, it will still bug you after you get married. If you can't let it go, don't get married.

If you're 'saving up' so you have enough money to get married, don't get married.

If you're afraid to get married, as many claim to be, then, don't get married.

If you love your fiancée more than you like her, don't get married.

If you aren't your most free and open self around your fiancé, don't get married.

If you're a virgin but your fiancée isn't, and it bothers you enough that you're losing sleep, don't get married.

If you think that your fiancé is responsible for completing you, don't get married.

If you feel like you should get married because you're getting older and you want to have children before you turn a certain age, don't get married.

If you're getting married because you want to help your fiancée, don't get married.

If you're getting married because you want to fix something about your fiancé, don't get married.

If you realize at any time prior to the wedding that you are no longer in love with your fiancée, don't get married.

If you have questions about your sexual identity, discuss them with your fiancé. If you can't, don't get married.

If you're getting married because you have to, don't get married.

If you think marriage is an answer to your problems, don't get married.

If your fiancée has physically, sexually, or mentally abused you at any time during your courtship and engagement, do not get married.

"The little lady was a dancer, and she stretched out both her arms, and raised one of her legs so high, that the tin soldier could not see it at all, and he thought that she, like himself, had only one leg. 'That is the wife for me,' he thought."

Hans Christian Andersen, *The Brave Tin Soldier*

Your touch, my face

It is a sweet remembrance
of half my life ago,
a sip, a sudden warmth
of flavor from a
waxen, antique candy:
very hard, very sweet.
A pew of hardened, praying souls,
heads lowered,
save one.
A sunflower drinking sun was
my face, your touch,
like one, serene, expressive breath,
the look of one
from that unlowered head,
the breath of that a breath of grace,
your touch, my face.

~Passion is important

It's one thing to feel something. It's another thing to cultivate that feeling for the rest of your life.

Chances are, you were brought together by the divinely inspired force people call chemistry, or spark, or attraction. It is also possible, as has been proven by societies the world over, that passion can be developed over time, as many successfully arranged marriages attest.

The Western ideal of falling in love has good intentions with often poor results. Once you've fallen, will you be able to get up? In other words, will the essential parts of your love last after the luster of romance has worn away?

Passion, and romance, are not synonymous. Romance has to do with the impractical and the ideal, with that sense of adventure borne from a new person or place. Passion has more to do with staying in love because passion is about love *and* suffering, the kind of experience that tempers and strengthens the connections which make your love real.

Practice your passion for each other. Talk about it often. Show it in a variety of ways. Learn how you express your passion, and learn the passion language of your spouse.

Understand that passion has as much to do with physical intimacy as it does with emotional closeness. Don't expect one to exist without the other. If you find your passion for each other waning, do something about it. Don't wait, and don't make excuses. Often, marriages need only the smallest jumpstart to reignite the fire.

Choose to suffer with and for each other. Find ways that your passion can alleviate your spouse's daily aches and pains. You'll be surprised at the increase of desire between yourselves, as well as the increase of your emotional well-being.

How you feel about each other is important. What you do, day after day about that feeling, is even more so.

"The mystic loved the Song of Songs because he saw there reflected, as in a mirror, the most secret experiences of his soul. The sense of a desire that was insatiable, of a personal fellowship so real, inward, and intense that it could only be compared with the closest link of human love, of an intercourse that was no mere spiritual self-indulgence, but was rooted in the primal duties and necessities of love."

Evelyn Underhill

Valentines Day 2002

Into the velvet smell of our love's birth
I threw my first self, my simple loving.
Like maddened frogs that dig into the earth,
I sought you solely. There was no shoving,
no coercion, no third mind: I craved you.
And in that craving, I found peace, stillness,
a calm that burns cool flames of hottest blue,
a welcome fever to this sweet illness.
So, if like lemmings, rushing to the shore,
I sometimes drown myself, my mind grown sick
with desire to drink you, to know you more,
be kind to me, you who turn my blood thick
with need. Your thinning antidote, your draught,
my only hope to right this mind gone aft.

~When you begin keeping track of what household chores you have done versus what your spouse has done, you have created an endlessly unhappy accounting firm, not a marriage.

Daily chores are a fact of life.

Unless they aren't.

Why expect that your spouse should do the dishes more often, when you could eat off paper plates?

You don't like paper plates? Then eat at a restaurant.

Restaurants aren't your thing? Move into a dormitory, and buy a meal plan.

You don't want to go to college? Join the Peace Corps and live in a village where they only have one pot for food, and one platter from which everyone eats, using their hands. They set the pot and the platter out in the field for the dogs to lick, after the meal is over.

You don't like dog slobber?

Then wash the dishes.

Don't let menial tasks degrade the sanctity of your marriage.

> *"When two people have a dispute, both are to blame. And therefore, a dispute will stop only when at least one person understands that he or she is guilty."*
>
> Leo Tolstoy

Come into this house

Come into this house! Its doors are wide,
Come in and dance until your burden sings,
this place where fools as geniuses abide.

Within these walls watch holiness collide
with everything that good, deep loving brings.
Come into this house. Its doors are wide

for common folk that sophists will deride.
Join in our search for undiscovered wings.
This place where fools as geniuses abide

is your house, too! For we make up the bride
of one whose back has borne the sting of stings.
Come into this house! Its doors are wide.

There are no secrets here; you need not hide
with costumes, hair-dos, baubles, scarves and rings.
This place where fools as geniuses abide

bids "Eat and drink with us! We've set aside
a place for you filled with awakenings.
Come into this house! Its doors are wide,
this place where fools as geniuses abide.

~You're not marrying a family, you're marrying into one. Honor each other's families, but don't let them walk all over you, or your spouse.

It seems like every newlywed should love his or her spouse's family. Often, this is true. Just as often, it isn't.

Your respective families contribute hugely to your relationship. They influence how you affect each other, in what you've learned to do, and not to do. These learned behaviors will surface eventually within your marriage, and they can be interesting, and challenging, to deal with.

Follow these guidelines:

1) Don't blame your husband's family for his behavior. It's not their fault.

2) Don't talk poorly about your wife's family, even if you can't stand them. It's painful for your wife, even if she can't stand them, too. You'll only hurt your marriage, and it makes it harder on both of you the next time you have to see them.

3) You don't have to love your husband's family, but you do have to honor them. Understand this difference.

4) Don't bring up your wife's family's dysfunctional qualities when you're having a disagreement with her. It creates a wedge between you, and it's not fair in any case.

5) Don't participate in holiday or vacation 'visiting games.' Decide what works best for your leisure plans and do it. Giving in to parental pressure only makes the situation worse. Be fair to yourselves, and try to

be fair to each other's families, even though it may be difficult, but don't do it at the cost of your relationship.

6) Living close to family can be both a joy and a challenge. Don't take them for granted either way.

7) Be clear, consistent, and gentle when dealing with each other's families. If you don't like something, say it with love. If you need something, say it with love. If you keep your mouth shut, and don't say anything, letting yourself stew, you will most likely not speak with love when the time comes to say how you feel. And it will come.

8) Don't allow your parents to talk poorly about your spouse. Gentle, timely correction of this inappropriate behavior is essential to the future of healthy family relations.

9) Understand that your husband's parents are from a different generation, and possibly a different geography as well. What may seem charming and unique in your husband may be irritating and unbearable in his parents. Expect this, and give them space, if necessary. Be forgiving.

10) A man shall leave his mother and a woman leave her home. Don't put up with parental interference in the workings of your marriage. It isn't right.

"…A man will leave his father and mother and be united to his wife, and the two will become one flesh. So they are no longer two, but one. Therefore what God has joined together, let man not separate."

Matthew 19:5-6

Thanksgiving Edict 2002

The Science Department of the World
has announced:

There will be no more Thanksgiving dinners with
bad relatives: the green bean chemistry between
passed dishes and helped selves has reached
toxic levels.

The following comparative analysis test
shall be administered to all
out-of-state family-type guests prior to household admission:
hot pads are to burns as
watermarks are to[coasterless drinking glasses];
and all eaters, laughter prone or no, must submit to
pre-meal auditory examinations (lip
smackers are not allowed to make
others
gag).

Table lengths shall be in direct proportion
to the spreading of unnecessary conversations
between appointed diners, with regard to their
passive-aggressive obsessions with hot rolls vs. the
placement of the butter dish.

Furthermore, those individuals who
choke on the string of the bean
will be subject to
continuing pharyngeal examinations, and in
no way shall any part or whole of the dinner be
revealed through either leftovers or any
other post-meal physical, and/or emotional,
releasings.

~If you don't like hard work, don't get married

It's not as if the hard work of marriage is the back breaking work of hoeing a hardened garden all by yourself, though it may feel like that sometimes. Working on a marriage is about finding ways to make the good practice of your love more like a pleasurable routine than a duty. It's about making choices that create harmony, not acrimony.

Child care, laundry, family reunions, bill paying, lawn mowing: all these and more are the outer tasks that will reflect your inner marital peace, or lack thereof, when it's time to get things done. The work of marriage is the steadfast dedication and patience required to figure out how to 'do' your life, and how to enjoy it while you're doing it.

Take turns in the garden. Better yet, work together. Share the labors of your lives. Soon you will begin to look forward to the work of your relationship. For at the end of the day, a well-tilled garden bears delicious reward, and a hoe becomes a thing of beauty when the feast is on the table, ready to be shared.

"The spiritual marriage is like the water that falls from the heavens and unites with the water of rivers and springs in such a way that the earthly water can no longer be distinguished from the other; or it is like a little brook that enters the ocean, and there is lost; or again it is like a strong light which, divided, streams into a house through two windows, and there forms but one light."

St. Teresa of Avila

$ = $

$ \neq ♥

♥ \neq $

♥ + ♥ \neq $

$ = $

♥ + ♥ = ∞

$ \neq ☺

☺ \neq $

♥ + ♥ - $ \neq ☹, but

♥ + ♥ - $ can = ☹

☺ + ☺ ÷ $ always = ☹

"*Whoever has loved knows all that life contains of sorrow and joy.*"

George Sand

~Forgiveness is fun, and necessary, for a healthy marriage.

Some people easily let go of past hurts. Some do not. Inevitably, you will do and say things that hurt each other. Be thankful for these moments, as they open the door that invites forgiveness in to do its work, making your marriage richer.

Forgiveness builds. What was broken or damaged, after words of forgiveness, grows into something stronger than it originally was. It is rebuilt, and tougher than before. A bone is always stronger where it was first broken.

Forgiveness is eternal. In practicing it, every day, you begin both to better understand its mystery and to reap its full reward: everyone wins, and the winning continues with each new chance to forgive each other.

Forgiveness is clever. If you tell your wife you've forgiven her, but you haven't, you are the one who will be eaten up by whatever resentment you're harboring. So forgive her, and you'll feel better. It always works.

Forgiveness works in both big and small chunks. You can either forgive your husband daily, or in one lump of ongoing forgiveness for the future. Both work, though the latter often creates miraculous, lasting changes of behavior, as most bad boys continue their bad manners only to spite the nagging which they have come to regard as inevitable.

Forgiveness is amazing. Things always end up better than you could have imagined, because the forgiver is healed first.

Forgiveness is infectious. Practice forgiveness as if you're spreading a good illness. When it's your turn to be forgiven (and your turn will surely come), you'll already be a carrier of this lovely disease, making you better able to receive it.

Forgiveness is fun. The more you do it, the more you'll look forward to it.

Forgiveness makes things easier, unless you don't do it. So do it, and grant yourself the easiest marriage on earth.

Who doesn't want that?

"Forgive us our sins, as we forgive those who sin against us."

Jesus

Carol and burden

From my window,
one sliver of lake.
Treacherous.
In the invisible land of ground beneath the waves,
what breaks me, remains.
Traitor.
(There is a land of desire. It is blank.)
Call me. Remove the veil. Stand.
Is there another way
(I cannot lead you down a logical path. There is no
sense in it. It is not true.)
please.

The difference of snow
through any one window
is just

as if any one door might not be
the land beyond once believed

I have a tango on a 78.
(*Jalousie*)
I have a 78 record record-player.
I listen alone
(I cannot mistake my need for you to read this
as
something impure. I dare not,
for surviving's sake.)
only.
A record is a one-eyed window
with singing wounds, always cold.

Breakable.
Love is a needle.
One eye severely unclear, one not.
Scratches heal, scars don't.
There is no heat in memory unless we grant it.

The difference of snow
through any one window
is just

as if any one door might not be
the land beyond once believed

By the lake
near a certain cold stone,
the grit, just before the lake's tongue
(I can only fall on you like rain. There is
no other way.)
is a warning. Teeth.
A stroll in the name of love,
particularly a stroll next to a shoreline,
cannot be hidden or reversed.
(Can a lake feel rain, can a lake answer)
No matter the manner or the means,
ours is the transformation.
The stone remains.
From my window.
At the lake's lip.
Jalousie.

The difference of snow
through any one window
is just

as if any one door might not be
the land beyond once believed

The hardness of true winter is easy.
My 8th floor apartment has this same easiness.
What is to come is softened by what is.
This is misunderstood, as winter is.
Heatlessness softens the heat to come.
This is true.
Heat never broke a thing.
Brokenness
(The land of desire is white. No.
Colorless from too much.)
is true.
From my window, everything is softer until
floor one's bottom part.
That is hard, and very easy to understand.
This is true winter's easiness.
A tango cannot escape
its record without
love, if love be a needle.
(A frozen lake is safer, sometimes.)
What is colder and harder than a needle?
This is easy.

The difference of snow
through any one window
is just

as if any one door might not be
the land beyond once believed

The doctor burned my warts
with liquid nitrogen.
I understand this riddance.
(A lake is a window into something deeper.
This is the promise I feel. It scares me.)
It scares me.

The difference of snow
through any one window
is just

as if any one door might not be
the land beyond once believed

My cat cowers in the corner by the front door.
He does not know
there is no touching when thunder is involved.
After a storm, as the steam rises off the streets,
snow having softened into rain,
(My heart dwells in the invisible land there between)
there is no telling where it will all end
and there is no strangeness in the changes of my window.
After a storm, he lays on the sill in the sun.
(Your heart is my desire
and nothing else. There
is no other thing.)
Sweet beast.

The difference of snow
through any one window
is just

as if any one door might not be
the land beyond once believed

~Infidelity comes in all shapes and sizes

It is no fun live in the fear of your marriage capsizing from an extra-marital affair. Nonetheless, it bears saying: infidelity comes in all shapes and sizes. Beware the Internet, the workplace, the church, your friends, and your family; anyone and anything that violates the emotional and/or physical sanctity of your marriage.

An affair doesn't have to involve another person. You, or your spouse, in the name of lots of ideas that seem upright and worthy, can be unfaithful to each other through misplaced loyalties, poorly aligned work habits and schedules, varying priorities of time, money, leisure or accomplishment. The solution is talking. If your spouse will engage in dialogue with you regarding your concerns, hooray for you. If he or she won't, seek professional help.

Don't wield the threat of counseling, however, as an emotional weapon. Never give ultimatums: if your spouse won't talk, don't give up, but don't turn it into a battle. If your spouse won't attend counseling, go by yourself. If you learn from your counseling sessions, don't throw that knowledge back in your spouse's face. Be gentle, take time, and rest in the covenant that you made with each other on your wedding day. And don't give up.

Dialogue is the key word. It only ever works like this: one person talks, the other listens. This simple fact is ignored by many couples whose talk is too much yelling, too much banter, too much of the same harping that lead to the infidelity in the first place.

Don't be spooked by the possibilities. Don't be fooled by them either.

"Nearly all marriages, even happy ones, are mistakes: in the sense that almost certainly (in a more perfect world, or even with a little more care in this imperfect one) both partners might be found more suitable mates. But the real soul-mate is the one you are married to."

J.R.R. Tolkien

Men & Women: a short oratorio

Recit.-   (Radames)
        Here's Egyptian costumes.
        Here's singers, a curtain. Hey.
        It's Aida.
        Do we make it or do we do it?

Chorus- (Priestesses)
        Aida is everywhere: she liveth in men's hearts.
        Right in their cheap, poopy, 4th of July mainstreet parades
        Or in the nonspeaking way they wordlessly talk not at all;
        In their dumb handshakes; stiff, crispy and skinless. They
        Always want to touch her. They couldn't.
        Aida will not be touched, only seen, heard,
        Smelt.
        Touch is for everyone else.

Recit.-   (Radames)
        Here's elephants, some
        Priesties.
        Fat Ethiopians. That's funny.
        Hey, sad lady. Can I
        fix it?

Aria-   (Aida)
        Aida beggeth your attention, asketh:
        When did your belt-clipped, vibrating phones turn into
        self-dialed love-note machines?
        Where have all your showers gone?
        Why tap Morse-code love letters on your
        remotes of control?
        When will you ever learn?

Duetto- (Radames & Aida)
   Radames: Here's a tomb.
   Aida: Here sealeth we our fates.
   Radames: Yeah.

~Checklist

1. Don't avoid conflict. Fighting, within gracious boundaries (see #3), can help reestablish both the passion and the understanding of your relationship. Avoiding conflict for too long means bad things later in your married life. A pebble or two dropped in the river won't stop it from flowing, but ten years of pebbles will.

2. Remember that your spouse will change and grow, and so will you. There will be parts of you that you recognize from your first time together and parts that you don't. Cherish both, and leave room for what's to come. Grow together (see #4), but don't strangle each other. Every plant needs repotting now and then.

3. Speak to one another with an awareness of what your face, your body, (see #5) and your voice come across like. Though it isn't easy, practice insistent but gentle communication at all times. It takes experience to know how to talk to one another, learning what kind of approach your spouse best receives. Set time limits for conflicts, and stick to them.

4. Marriages are like gardens: they need weeding and watering and hoeing. They also need time to lay fallow (see #7). Keep your eye on the season of your love and be ready to lend a hand when necessary. And remember: excessive talk about weeds, with anyone else but your spouse, is emotional infidelity. Sharing with a friend is one thing, but disparaging your spouse is something to be avoided.

5. Your bodies are just as important to take care of as your hearts and minds. Encourage each other in love to eat well, rest well, work and play well. Give each other space (see #2) when it comes to differences

in lifestyle choices. Different bodies thrive on different things. Honor these differences, and don't nag.

6. Don't be an ass. Assume nothing about your spouse. As people aren't books, it never works to read them. Ask. Query. Question. And do it all with love (see #8). You'd be surprised how many people love to answer questions about themselves that are posed in gentleness and sincerity.

7. Everyone needs some time alone now and then. Allow for this. Because marriage is all about learning to operate together (see #9), it's important that each of you have time to meditate and reflect without the other. You will always come back refreshed, and your relationship will be renewed.

8. Almost every problem you will have with each other stems from three things: A) not feeling loved, B) not feeling loved, and C) not feeling loved. When your spouse hurts you, it's probably because he or she is feeling hurt, too. So have some fun (see #10) and be a radical love freak: reverse the cycle of hurt, and compliment him. Praise her. Hug her. Kiss him. Shower your spouse with love. You'll feel better, too.

9. Don't speak for each other, ever. It is a lovely thing (when friends or acquaintances ask "Could you and your wife do *this* or *that*") to say "Let me check, and get back to you." It's a bit trickier with family members, who are often guilty of assuming (see #6) lots of things about you. But consistency with your team approach builds both your compatibility and your communication skills.

10. Enjoy life. Take risks. Challenge each other in loving support. Place yourselves in unusual situations. Dream together and act upon your dreams. You'll have a few conflicts (see #1) between yourselves or

others, but it will be worth it. You'll feel alive, and your relationship will grow.

"There is nothing nobler and more admirable than when two people who see eye to eye keep house as man and wife, confounding their enemies and delighting their friends."

Homer

Being married/why

It's going to feel like a lie, this whole
love/marriage Americana crap.
The old simple retarded reality of a
full-service dingaling fill-me-up nuptial stop simply isn't
the truth.

But you've got wedding in the dish and in the suds and
wedding in stupid fridge magnets.
Wedding in the beaten, sloping loveseat that
won't hold two.
Wedding in the olive jar turned juice glass and
wedding in the toast and the eggs even a dog wouldn't chew.

Teach your eyes the old photos.
Shove new love notes in your old mouth: don't swallow.
The drip, and the silence,
from your eyes, from your mouth,
is reality.
Trust that.

~Excluding the mountaintops and the valleys, your married life will directly the reflect the everyday qualities of your engagement. Open your eyes to the truth of who you both are, and do it now.

It is understandable if you have been frightened by this small, silly book. Largely gleaned from the unfettered mouths of the successfully married, its words are terse and its advice direct. Married people have a lot to say, and the crushing force of this waterfall of wisdom is too strong an irrigation for the tender sprout of the newly engaged, leaving the young, roots of your fresh love feeling raw and exposed. But at the very least, it will provoke discussion, and talking is the gas that makes the lovemobile get moving.

Self-examination, however, is essential before making the most important decision of your life. Hopefully, this book will help you in that process.

You are embarking on a spiritual journey, very much like what Anthony de Mello describes as an ascending staircase. The step from which you have just lifted your foot disappears the moment you leave it. The step you are about to take is not yet visible, but it is there.

You are stepping into the unknown, but you are doing it together. And that's what marriage is.

"Keep your eyes wide open before marriage, and half-shut afterwards."

Benjamin Franklin

About the Author

Joseph Byrd has been a school teacher, a nanny, a choral librarian, and a live-in supervisor of developmentally disabled adults. From 1996–97 he traveled with *Open Forum*, a discussion group that dialogued with high school students in former East Berlin, and in 1996 he was an Associate Artist in Poetry at the Atlantic Center for the Arts in Florida under Joy Harjo. He lives in Holland, Michigan with his wife and two daughters, working as Director of Celebration Ministries at Zion Lutheran Church, where he currently serves as Artistic Director of the *Upper Room Theatre*, which he founded in 2005. He is a novice in the Order of Ecumenical Franciscans.

978-0-595-39575-0
0-595-39575-9